American Vampire

VAMPIRE

VOLUME SEVEN

Scott Snyder Writer

Rafael Albuquerque

Matías Bergara Artists

Dave McCaig Colorist

Steve Wands Letterer

Rafael Albuquerque
Collection Cover Art

American Vampire created by
Scott Snyder and
Rafael Albuquerque

AMERICAN VAMPIRE VOLUME 7
Published by DC Comics. Compilation Copyright © 2015 Scott Snyder
and DC Comics. All Rights Reserved. Originally published in single magazine
form in AMERICAN VAMPIRE: SECOND CYCLE 1-5 © 2014 Scott Snyder
and DC Comics. All Rights Reserved. All characters, their distinctive likenesses
and related elements featured in this publication are trademarks of DC Comics.
Vertigo is a trademark of DC Comics. The stories, characters and incidents
featured in this publication are entirely fictional. DC Comics does not read or
accept unsolicited ideas, stories or artwork.

DC Comics, 4000 Warner Blvd., Burbank, CA 91522
A Warner Bros. Entertainment Company.
Printed in the USA. First Printing. ISBN: 978-1-4012-5432-2

Library of Congress Cataloging-in-Publication Data

Snyder, Scott, author.
    American Vampire volume seven / Scott Snyder, author ; Rafael
Albuquerque, artist.
       pages cm
    ISBN 978-1-4012-5432-2 (paperback)
    1. Vampires—Comic books, strips, etc. 2. Graphic novels. I.
Albuquerque, Rafael, 1981- illustrator. II. Title.

PN6727.S555A49 2014
741.5'973—dc23

                        2014034203

PEFC Certified

Printed on paper from
sustainably managed
forests and controlled
sources

PEFC/29-31-75   www.pefc.org

AMERICAN VAMPIRE

Texas/Mexico border. Near Juarez.

BOOM

FUCK... ≥COUGH≤ FUCK YOU...

...AND THE HORSE YOU RODE IN ON, MAN.

"WHAT DID I DO BEFORE? DID MY PARENTS USED TO LIVE HERE? WAS I EVER ARRESTED?"

WHAT SHE *WANTS*, BLESS HER HEART, IS TO KNOW WHO I AM. TO KNOW SHE'S *SAFE* WITH ME. NO DARK CORNERS FOR SURPRISES.

HOW BADLY I WANT TO GIVE HER THAT, TOO. TO JUST TELL HER, FACT AFTER FACT THE WAY SHE *WANTS* THEM. ADMITTEDLY, THOUGH, IT'D BE A LOT TO ABSORB BETWEEN HERE AND HER ROOM, AND SHE'S HAD A LONG DAY TO SAY THE LEAST.

WHAT AM I SUPPOSED TO SAY TO HER? MY REAL NAME? PEARL JONES. MY AGE? SIXTY-FIVE. THAT'S RIGHT, *SIXTY*-FIVE.

"SEE, MAY, I WAS AN ACTRESS IN HOLLYWOOD IN 1925 WHEN I WAS KILLED BY VAMPIRES. THE DRACULA KIND, YES.

"LUCKILY, THOUGH, I WAS SAVED BY A STRANGER, AND REBORN AS A NEW KIND OF MONSTER, A STRONGER KIND THAT CAN WALK IN THE SUN. ABOMINUS AMERICANA. AN *AMERICAN* VAMPIRE."

THE GUEST ROOM'S DOWN HERE. USED TO BE A STORM SHELTER, BUT MY FATHER EXPANDED IT DURING THE NUCLEAR SCARES.

IS IT *DARK* DOWN THERE?

NO. IT'S SAFE, I PROMISE. NOW COME ON...

"...YOU MIGHT AS WELL BE A MILLION MILES FROM NOWHERE."

I'M STILL AMAZED NO ONE'S FOUND THE DAMN THING AFTER ALL THIS TIME.

WE PUT IT HERE IN 1876, ME AND THE BOYS. SEPARATED IT FROM ITS PULLMAN AND JUST DRAGGED THE FUCKER OFF THE PACIFIC LINE INTO THE DESERT.

TOOK US NEARLY TWENTY HORSES TO HAUL IT JUST A FEW MILES. HALF OF THEM DIED EN ROUTE, THAT HEAT. YOU COULD HEAR THEIR HEARTS BURST.

ONCE WE GOT IT HERE, RONNIE JEEKS BLASTED A CRATER, AND WE SANK THE BASTARD. BURIED IT, WHEELS TO ROOF.

IT WAS OUR OWN HOLE IN THE WALL. A HIDEOUT INVISIBLE TO ANYONE BUT US.

A HIGH-STYLE TRAIN CAR, BURIED IN THE GROUND.

WE USED THE PLACE FOR YEARS. IF WE EVER GOT SEPARATED, WE'D MEET BACK AT THE TRAIN. HELL, WE USED TO JOKE THAT OUR *GHOSTS* WOULD GATHER HERE ONE DAY. JEEKSIE. THE BLACKMOUTH BOYS. BACK AT THE TRAIN.

NOW WHO THE FUCK SAID YOU CAN'T GO HOME?

HEY HEY, KITTY. MISS ME?

ORANGE, MARTY. GODDAMN ORANGE.

AMERICAN VAMPIRE SECOND CYCLE PART TWO
WRITER SCOTT SNYDER   ARTIST RAFAEL ALBUQUERQUE
COLORS DAVE McCAIG LETTERS STEVE WANDS
COVER BY RAFAEL ALBUQUERQUE

"RELAYS HOW?"

"TRAVELS AROUND, THEN COMES BACK HERE EVERY TWO MONTHS. THE INFORMATION IS IN THE SUIT HE WEARS."

"THE COLOR, THE DESIGN, IT'S *CODED* FOR US. LOOK OUT AT THE AUDIENCE. IT'S FULL OF VMS MEMBERS FROM AROUND THE COUNTRY."

AND WHAT DOES HIS SUIT SAY NOW?

ORANGE IS *DANGER.* BUT THE DESIGN...THE STORMY WAVES ON THE CUFFS. SOMETHING BIG IS COMING. SOMETHING *BAD.*

LISTEN...PEARL. WE GO BACK. YOU, ME AND HENRY, REST HIS SOUL. HELL, YOU MADE ME WHAT I AM. I HAVE *YOUR* BLOOD RUNNING THROUGH MY VEINS. I'M ASKING YOU AS A FRIEND...

...TO JOIN UP WITH US. THE *VASSALS* COULD USE YOUR HELP. AND MORE THAN THIS, I'M WORRIED ABOUT YOU, GIRL. WHAT YOU'RE DOING, HELPING OUR KIND ON THE RUN FROM THE *CARPATHIANS,* IT'S A GOOD THING. BUT IT CAN'T *LAST.* SOONER OR LATER, THE BIGGER STORM IS GOING TO LAND ON YOU.

THANKS, CAL. BUT I'M FROM KANSAS. I'M USED TO WEATHERING STORMS.

"TO HEAD INTO DARKNESS.. INTO COLD EMPTY DARKNESS..."

YOU CAN START **OVER.** I HAVE THE LOCATIONS OF NESTS OF EACH OF YOUR **SPECIES,** TOO. KILLIAN, YOU'RE IN VANCOUVER. LUCIA, YOU GET **WARM** WEATHER. I'LL LET YOU OPEN IT. AND TRAPP--

WILL YOU COME **VISIT?**

WE'LL SEE, OK?

WHAT ABOUT YOU, THOUGH, PEARL?

WHAT ABOUT ME, **WHAT,** HON?

WHAT'S GOING TO HAPPEN TO YOU?

I MEAN, YOU HELP US FIND NEW HOMES WITH OUR OWN KIND. PLACES WE CAN START OVER, SAFE FROM THE CARPATHIANS.

FROM WHATEVER'S **CHASING** US.

BUT YOU... YOU'RE JUST HERE, **ALONE.** DON'T YOU GET...I DON'T KNOW... LONELY?

SOMETIMES. SURE. IT'S FUNNY, MY HUSBAND--

YOU WERE MARRIED? WHAT SPECIES WAS HE?

HOMO SAPIENS, ACTUALLY. HIS NAME WAS HENRY.

WAIT. YOU NEVER **TURNED** HIM? DID YOU GUYS FALL OUT OF LOVE OR GET DIVORCED OR SOMETHING?

≥SIGH≤ HEH. NO, LUCIA. I LOVED HIM 'TIL THE END. AND HE LOVED ME, LUCKILY. WE WERE TOGETHER NEARLY *THIRTY* YEARS. I WANTED TO TURN HIM. BELIEVE ME, IT WAS THE HARDEST THING I'VE EVER *NOT* DONE.

BUT IN THE END, I THINK LIVING HIS ONE LIFE WAS ENOUGH FOR HIM. AND HE SEEMED TO BELIEVE, FOR WHATEVER REASON, THAT I HAD SOME *BIGGER* PURPOSE IN LIFE.

AFTER HE DIED, THOUGH...THE TRUTH IS, I JUST DIDN'T WANT TO *FIGHT* ANY MORE. I DIDN'T WANT TO SEE ANY MORE *HORRORS.*

"SO I CAME *HOME,* AND ONE DAY, I WAS IN A STORE IN TOPEKA, AND I SAW THIS SCARED WOMAN. I KNEW SHE WAS A *VAMPIRE,* AND THAT SHE WAS RUNNING, AND SO I TOOK HER IN. AND THAT STARTED IT.

"SOME DAYS I WONDER IF HENRY WOULD APPROVE. I KNOW HE'D LOVE YOU ALL, BUT I WONDER, IF HE WERE ALIVE, IF HE'D JUST TELL ME TO *BURN* THE FIELDS. JUST SET THEM ON FIRE AND MOVE ON."

I JUST DON'T--

BRING BRING

HELLO?

PEARL! PEARL YOU HAVE TO LISTEN TO ME!

CAL? SLOW DOWN! WHAT'S THE MATTER?

"THEY FLEW US DOWN A HOLE IN THESE...CLIFFS, SOME OLD MINE, MAYBE? I DON'T KNOW.

"WE WENT SO DEEP, THOUGH. LIKE WE DROPPED FOR HOURS...

"SO DEEP I COULD FEEL THE AIR WEIGHING DOWN, FULL OF WHITE DAMP. BLACK DAMP. FIRE DAMP. I'M TALKING *DEEP* DOWN MINE GASES. SULFIDE AND CARBON. ENOUGH TO KILL ANYONE NOT DEAD ALREADY.

"EVERYONE FROM THE BUS WAS THERE. SCREAMING, BEING PULLED THIS WAY AND THAT.

"AND THERE WERE...THINGS DOWN THERE. A *LOT* OF THEM.

"I RAN AS FAST AS I COULD.

"RAN FOR MILES UNTIL I FOUND A CAR.

"DROVE NON-STOP 'TIL I GOT *HERE*."

"BUT THAT'S IT, *SKINNER*. WHY HERE?"

"THE PEOPLE ON THAT BUS, DOLLY. THEY KNEW ABOUT *YOU*. PLENTY WERE HEADED HERE. THEY WERE RUNNING FROM HIM, HERE. NOT THE CARPATHIANS. HELL, SOME OF THEM MIGHT HAVE *BEEN* CARPATHIANS."

"I DON'T UNDERSTAND."

"WHATEVER'S DOWN THERE, PEARL, IT KNOWS ABOUT *YOU*. I COULD FEEL IT. IT'S COMING FOR YOU."

"YOU CAME ALL THE WAY HERE TO WARN ME, SKINNER?"

AMERICAN VAMPIRE SECOND CYCLE PART FOUR

WRITER **SCOTT SNYDER** ARTIST **RAFAEL ALBUQUERQUE**
COLORS **DAVE McCAIG** LETTERS **STEVE WANDS**
COVER BY **RAFAEL ALBUQUERQUE**

AT FIRST GLANCE, IT LOOKED LIKE A BOOK.

JUST PAPER AND DIRTY LEATHER. FIFTY PAGES OF PRESSED LINEN, NOT EVEN WOOD PULP, BUT *LINEN.* NEARLY A HUNDRED AND FIFTY YEARS OLD.

THE TRUTH IS, I DIDN'T THINK MUCH OF IT, WHEN I DISCOVERED IT ON OUR SHELVES.

IF I'D ONLY KNOWN WHERE IT WOULD LEAD ME...

AND TO THINK ASSESSING BOOKS IS WHAT I DO. IT'S MY JOB FOR THE *VASSALS* OF THE MORNINGSTAR, AN ANCIENT ORGANIZATION DEDICATED TO THE ERADICATION OF ALL MANNER OF ABOMINATIONS. MY NAME IS *GENE BUNTING,* AND FOR THE PAST DECADE, I'VE WORKED AS THEIR WEST COAST BOOKKEEPER.

STILL, I THOUGHT THE BOOK WAS JUST A BOOK, UNTIL I OPENED IT.

THANK GOD.

HELLO? HELLO, IS ANYONE THERE?

PUT CASH IN THE CASH CAN, I'LL TURN ON THE STANDING.

May 19th, 1850

WEALTH TO BE HA
Gentlemen of fortitude, a n
endeavor is being undertak
by the Royal Forkes Mini
Enterprise! One of the olde
mining companies in the wor
the proprietors of Royal Fork
are confident the area alo
Red Gum Creek in southe
Nevada to be rich in miner
wealth! We are looking for
few intrepid men, scientif
capitalists, to aid us in t
extraction of precious meta
Men of God, we will pay a doll
a week!

I was looking for quartz when Seb hurried over with a page torn out the newspaper. It was an advertisement and he was pushing it at me, panting, flushed with excitement.

"Take a look," he said, handing me the page, wet from his hand. I was hot and tired from wet panning all day. There was no shade along the Sacremento, but here was Seb, pushing a page of the Californian at me.

"Take a look at what?" I said. The company was called Royal Forkes and I'd never heard of it. It had an insignia like hair standing on end.

I saw nothing special in it and I told Seb so.

my pal Seb

"What are you, sun blind?" he said. He pointed to a spot on the advertisement I could barely read, as the sweat from his thumb had corrupted it. I looked closely and saw that it was the promise of a dollar a week pay.

I held the page out to him. "No one pays that," I said. "It's a trick."

"It's British coal, Dodger," he said. Dodgerman was my surname. Sebberton his. "British coal treats their people right. My father told me, if I ever got a chance to try British, I should. I'm telling you."

"Your father never mined a day in his life," I said. Seb took the advertisement back. "Look," he said. "We need to throw in with this. Hell, there's nothing for us here anyway."

I looked at the empty pan in my hands and then at Seb. He was my oldest friend. We'd met in a schoolhouse in St. Louis at nine years old, nearly ten years ago. He wanted to be a writer for the papers. Me, I wanted to be an illustrator. Our fathers were both tannery men and wanted us with them. Demanded it. But instead we'd set off together when the boom had begun, Two young men defying their fathers, off to find our fortune. Now here we were, in the mountains of California, no money, no prospects...

And so today we are on our way south to Nevada. We've spent every last cent on a coach down. The wheels are missing spokes and the fellow driving us looks like he will kill us in our sleep, but Seb is smiling from ear to ear.

Looking at him, I cannot help but be optimistic about what we might find.

THE BOOK MADE A LONG JOURNEY BEFORE COMING INTO MY POSSESSION.

IT'S BELIEVED THAT *HARRY HOUDINI* ACQUIRED IT IN HIS LATER TRAVELS, DEBUNKING SPIRITUALISTS ACROSS AMERICA. FOR A LONG TIME IT WAS SHELVED IN HIS *PRIVATE* COLLECTION, A LIBRARY OF THE OCCULT, AS "AN OBJECT FOR FURTHER STUDY."

UPON HIS DEATH, THE BOOK PASSED HANDS, UNTIL IT ENDED UP IN THE STUDY OF HOWARD PHILLIPS LOVECRAFT.

A FRIEND OF THE VASSALS, HOWARD DONATED THE BOOK TO US IN HIS LAST DAYS.

SINCE I DISCOVERED THE BOOK, I HAVEN'T KNOWN WHOM TO TRUST.

... AND THE CREEK SPLITS.

ALL RIGHT, ROYAL FORKES. LET'S DIG YOU UP.

We arrived at the Royal Forkes...

June 20th, 1850

We arrived at the Royal Forkes camp today, and I will say that the site is not what I expected.

It was early morning when we approached the camp. The odd thing was, after traveling nearly five hundred miles with us, our horses gave out not five miles from the camp. It was peculiar to be sure.

We were traveling lightly across the cracked, bright dirt, so close to camp we could almost see it, and suddenly the animals simply stopped. Mine halted first. It happened so abruptly I nearly fell. The beast froze, and, for a moment, touched its knees to the dirt, as though in protest. Seb's animal planted its feet as well.

After such a long journey, Seb and I were so glad to be near the site that we found the whole incident wildly humorous. Our horses giving out here, so close to our destination. We gave them water and tried to coax them, but they would not move. We were laughing, pulling on them, when we heard a voice behind us.

"Sirs," said the voice.

We turned to find a man standing along the creek. He was dressed as a gentleman, in vests, and he was strikingly handsome. He could not have looked more out of place in the Nevada desert.

His accent was evident. British, and Seb elbowed me in the ribs at the sound of it. "British coal"... he mouthed.

"My name is Joseph Pell," said the man, touching his own vest. "And as the assistant foreman of the Royal Forkes site, it's my honor and pleasure to welcome you both to camp. The site is just this way. Can I take anything for you?"

Seb and I exchanged a glance. What a voice. Like something forged from silver by the queen's metallurgist. He was a gentleman in the desert, asking to carry our bags.

Joseph Pell

"So kind of you," said Seb. And before I could protest, Seb had handed this man - Pell - his satchel. It was cumbersome, but Pell took it without so much as flinching.

He turned to me. "And yours, sir?" he said.

I wanted to keep it, but his hand was there, waiting, and I surrendered it.

"Let me thank you both for coming, on behalf of our foreman," he said, our bags hanging from his slender shoulders, heavy with equipment. He seemed unbothered. "If you'll follow me. I assure you we'll compensate you for the animals, if they've expired. Set them free, and don't trouble yourselves."

He turned and began walking away. Again Seb and I looked at each other. We had to restrain ourselves from laughing. What an oddity, this man, this desert, this situation...

But we followed him, our horses staying behind, watching us go.

The camp itself was a surprise for both Seb and myself. We had tried three mining camps back in the Sierras and all were raucous, filthy places. Men would work by day, drink at night, fight, curse, sing, fornicate, kill... Every tent its own flag planted on a claim. Little ragged countries, all at war with one another.

But the Royal Forkes site it... was like nothing either of us had encountered. Clean white tents. Lined up in a row... Like polished shoes.

At the end of the line of tents was a larger tent, exceedingly large in fact. It loomed above the row, its peak like a steeple poking high above the others. Its cloth was dark, nearly black.

Outside the white row of tents were miners, men like us. Except they were quiet and calm, sitting or standing by the flaps. Each watched our approach in silence, with a kind smile and a nod. I wondered if the camp had religion.

Pell showed us to our tent, which was clean and spacious as the others. Better than anything either of us could have hoped for. After placing our bags inside, Pell reached inside his vest and produced two shiny objects.

the foreman's tent

The disks sat in his palm, catching the light from outside. "In advance of your good work," he said. Seb took his right away but it took me a moment to understand what it was I was looking at. It was bright and gleaming. A dollar coin. I looked at Pell. He was smiling at me and I was struck again by his handsomeness. "We believe in treating our workers right," he said. "That's what the foreman believes, I should say."

And just then I felt a sudden wave of gratitude rise in me. Towards Seb, for bringing me the advertisement, for this gentleman carrying our bags. I could draw you a sketch of my own heart, swollen. "Please tell the foreman back in jolly old England how much we appreciate it," I said. "If we could take back the revolution, we would." He smiled even more broadly. His eyes were a cloudy blue, nearly white. Pools of water in a desert. "You can thank him yourself sometime," said Pell. "He's staying here. His tent is at the end of the row, see?" I looked through the flaps of our tent at that large black structure in the distance, the top rising above the rest, dark against the sky.

"He's with his wife," said Pell. "She's with child. Not easy out here, as you can imagine. He's a devoted man." I thanked the foreman silently. Pell bid us goodbye and told us to explore the camp, sleep, whatever we wanted to do. I wanted to rest but it was early, and Seb encouraged me to explore the camp with him. We couldn't stop smiling, glancing at each other as we walked the rows of perfect tents... Oddly, all the other miners were gone now, presumably having gone inside their tents to rest. It was like Seb and I were the only men around, the whole camp built for us.

We walked past the tents, past the well, the creek, out into the desert, where the beginnings of the shaft itself had been sunk. The others hadn't gotten very far, but even so, the mouth was wide and deep. An impressive start. We were just about to walk back to our tent when Seb took my arm.

"It is a bit strange," he said.
"If it's a dream, don't wake me," I said.
"No," he said, "there's no material for extraction. All this," he said, gesturing to the rigging, the narrow elevator, "it's for digging a hole. Not pulling anything out of that hole."
"Like I said, don't wake me."
I tapped his head with my coin. "If they want us to dig a hole, so be it. We can do it, then we'll be gone with our pay, never to be seen again!"

The Hole

July 5th, 1850

here's something wrong with this place. . . That's what Seb believes.
e's become increasingly fearful these past days. As I said, he has
en suspicious from the very first day. Lately, though, the things he's
magining. . . At night he spends hours peeking through the flaps
the foreman's black tent at the end of the row, hoping to catch a
impse. He was always the more excitable of the two of us,
ough. Full of wild humors, his father liked to say. I love Seb
r it, but his father used to give him soda waters to
lm him down.

ill, I admit, there is strangeness here. Seb's initial observation
out the site was correct. Royal Forkes does seem more interested in
gging a hole than extracting anything from it. We dig straight down,
essurizing the water, blasting away what we can, then chopping,
opping. We blast now and then. No diagonal shafts, nothing to buttress
is one. No exploring. Just straight down. We're getting deep, fast.
ere are sorts of damps in the air already. Black damp. . .
skunk damp.

nd yes, a single hole, directly down is odd to be sure, but even so. . .
rhaps there's some other purpose the company wants to keep
ivate. A geological survey is my guess. Something bigger
an just mining for wealth. When asked, everyone on site,
cluding Pell, claims the shaft is being sunk to
tract precious metal, but I saw what I'm sure
s silver the other day, and we kept
king the hole, right past it. No one
med to care when I made mention of it.

e'll examine all we've got when we
deep enough, good sir," said
ll. Then he put a hand on my
oulder. It was oddly heavy. "I
ar you're an artist. I'd love to see
ur illustrations some time. You keep
em in that book of yours?"

e other day Pell asked them to pour a
nd of red dust - like brick dust - around
e edge of the hole. He said it was an old
ck to add moisture and harden the lips. But
r a trick of which I've never heard, and I say it
es look strange, like a ring of blood around a
ping black mouth...

l of this, though, I truly believe it's all of Seb's nonsense poisoning
thoughts. The full truth is, he has come to see all sorts of paranoid
nsense around us. He says the other miners are watching us. He believes something has
en done to them so he has stopped eating anything but bread. "I can see the makings of bread,"
says. I see him stare at the mining company symbol sometimes as though he detects evil in it.
keep telling myself it's only a few more weeks, though. At the rate we're digging, the hole will be insupportably
deep in a matter of days. And the money. . .
We've made more in a few weeks than we would
in a year.

I have the coins stacked next to this journal
right now. It's nearly midnight, and their shine in
the pale moonlight coming in the flaps. . . the flaps
letting in light because Seb is peeking out again.
Staring at the black tent at the end of the row.
He is whispering something to himself. I cannot
hear what.

I'd lay a hand on him if I didn't think he'd jump.

July 19th, 1850

Seb ran tonight. He just fled, all at once. I tried to dissuade him, but there was no reasoning with him. He was like a man possessed.

His decision to flee was apparently prompted by something he saw moments ago. Over the course of the past few nights, there've been screams from the foreman's tent. His wife, screaming in pain. Of course, we all assumed it was the start of her labor. But the screams went on all night. In the morning, they stopped, only to start again when the sun was down. Yesterday morning, again they halted abruptly. And last night, at almost the instant the sun sank below the horizon, they began again. Shrieks, blood-curdling. Every few minutes, one spiraling up into the sky, the pitch growing higher and higher as the night wore on, growing impossibly high, inhumanly so. Like the scream of a sheep, or a goat being torn apart.

Seb and I lay awake, listening. I was about to talk to him, to see how he was holding up, when he stood, angrily, and stormed off.

"Where are you going?" I said.

"To meet our foreman and his wife, of course" he said, and then he was through the flaps before I could stop him.

"Seb!" I called after him. "Seb, wait!" But he wouldn't hear it. It was so dark that night I lost sight of him before he neared the black tent. But I could see the tent itself, blacker than the night sky, peeking up above us all.

I started out of the tent, but then something seized in me and I stayed put. Why didn't I follow my friend? Was I afraid? I don't know, but I didn't follow him, and moments later, Seb returned and began to pack - frantically.

I asked him what he'd seen but he wouldn't say. He was shaking, his face pale. He seemed to see nothing but his belongings. He'd barely filled his bag when he slung it over his shoulder.

He looked at me.

"I saw him," he said. "The foreman. And the. . . the wife. We need to leave. Now."

I told him to stop, to talk this through a moment.

But then, before I could say anything more, he was gone. My friend. Vanished into the night. It was only later I noticed he hadn't even taken his coins. He'd left them all in the tent. A small fortune.

I only pray he makes it where he wants to go. I worry he was right. I worry I should run too, before it's too late. I worry one of these times. . .

...I'll go down in that hole, and won't come back up.

JUST A LITTLE FARTHER, GENE...

...YOU'RE *ALMOST* THERE.

ALL YOUR SUSPICIONS, ALL THE RESEARCH THESE PAST WEEKS... HIDDEN FROM THE OTHERS. ROYAL FORKES. THE *INSIGNIA*, HOW IT CONTAINS THE OLDER AKKADIAN MARK. THE SEVEN TONGUES. OR "TONGS." THE *PITCHFORK*, THE SPECIES THE THING MAKES BEFORE EMERGING...

IT WAS PUT DOWN *HERE*, YOU KNOW IT. BY THE ROYAL FORKES, JUST LIKE IT SAYS IN THE BOOK.

IT'S ALL TRUE.

A LITTLE FARTHER AND YOU'LL PROVE IT. YOU'LL HAVE ENOUGH TO SHOW AGENT BOOK, ASSUMING YOU CAN TRUST HER. YOU CAN, GENE. YOU CAN. YOU KNOW HER. SHE'S A FRIEND.

Seb came back two nights ago...

July 21st 1859

Seb came back two nights ago... Or rather, whatever replaced him came back. I must write faster, as I don't have much time. He'd been gone for two nights when it happened. I'd actually become hopeful that he'd made it, escaped from camp. I'd taken to imagining him arriving back in St. Louis, tired and dirty, but alive. I imagined him going straight into Roscoe's, walking down the barrel drains and tanners and finding our fathers and hugging them both. Or maybe he'd make it, maybe he'd make it to New York. Maybe he'd write about me, and I'd live on in his stories. I was thinking these thoughts, half asleep, when he came back. Or when I noticed he was simply there.

I heard a stirring, a rustling sound like dirt scraping, and when I looked, he was lying there in his bed. Like he'd never gone anywhere. His eyes were open, and he was staring at me. He looked filthy, but his expression was calm and peaceful.

"Seb?" I said. "Seb, what happened?"

"Nothing at all, Dodger," he said. He lay there, staring at me, unblinking.

The woman's screams from the tent started again just then. EEEEEEEEEeeeeeeeee!!!!!!!

This thing says it's Seb but it's not. It watches me at night.

This morning the Seb thing pissed and shat itself and didn't even move.

It just smiled.

July 24th 1859

I know this will likely be my last entry.

This morning the Seb thing, moments ago, without warning, it got up and walked out of the tent. I was shocked. Why had it left? I noticed then that the foreman's wife - her screams sounded louder, closer than usual. They'd become commonplace, like the howling of the wind. I peeked out of the tent and what I saw. . .

She was not with child, but with something else, stretched to bursting. . .

She hung from a bed built upside down.
Her cries were terrible, ecstatic, shrieks
of glee for what was coming.
I wanted to scream, to run, but I
stood frozen to the spot.
That's when I saw him. The
foreman himself...

He had his back to me, but I knew it
was him. He stood taller than the
other men, looming like his tent had loomed
over the others.

I had a sense that he was very old. Older than this place. Older than the dirt.

I had a sense of something timeless and evil and then he turned to me...

I could feel my pulse in my hands, throbbing.

He smiled. A slow smile that stretched too widely across his face.
His whole face seemed a mouth.

And then it was as though the spell was broken and I rushed inside
the tent.

I write this knowing I will not escape.

I will die here.

We have dug a pit.

A Nest for something. I have no heart left. No spirit.

Supplies come in every week, and I will try to hide this journal in the
rigging. It will likely be found and burned. But even so, I will try.
And above all...

... I beg whoever finds it never to come here. And to remember me as
I was, not as I am now, a wasted, haunted shell of myself.

My name was William Dodgeman of Chicago.

This was my face.

This was my face.

This was my face...

LET GO! GET OFF!

CLIMB, GENE! YOU HAVE IT!

JUST KEEP--

AGH!

WHAT IN...

NO. NO, NO...

MEN WORKING IN THE PARK

American Vampire #5 layouts by Matías Bergara

American Vampire #5 page 3 color study by Matías Bergara

American Vampire #5 page 17 color study by Matías Bergara

American Vampire #5 unused cover by Matías Bergara

Scott Snyder has written comics for both DC and Marvel, including the best-selling series BATMAN and SWAMP THING, and is the author of the story collection *Voodoo Heart*. He teaches writing at Sarah Lawrence College and Columbia University. He lives on Long Island with his wife, Jeanie, and his sons Jack and Emmett. He is a dedicated and un-ironic fan of Elvis Presley.

Rafael Albuquerque was born in Porto Alegre, Brazil, and has been working in the American comic book industry since 2005. Best known for his work on the *Savage Brothers*, BLUE BEETLE and SUPERMAN/BATMAN, he has also published the creator-owned graphic novels *Crimeland* (2007) and *Mondo Urbano* (2010).

Matías Bergara is an up-and-coming artist from Montevideo, Uruguay. He has previously drawn Zenescope Entertainment's *Grimm Fairy Tales Presents Demons: The Unseen*, and is currently working with BOOM! Studios on *Sons of Anarchy* and *Sleepy Hollow*. AMERICAN VAMPIRE: SECOND CYCLE is his first title for Vertigo.

Dave McCaig was raised by bears in the Canadian tundra and has since pinballed his way across North America to his current digs in New York City. He is probably best known for his work coloring SUPERMAN: BIRTHRIGHT, NORTHLANDERS, and ADAM STRANGE, and as color supervisor on *Batman: The Animated Series*.

FROM THE *NEW YORK TIMES* #1 BESTSELLING
AUTHOR OF *BATMAN VOL. 1: THE COURT OF OWLS*

SCOTT SNYDER
with RAFAEL ALBUQUERQUE and STEPHEN KING

**AMERICAN VAMPIRE
VOL. 2**

with RAFAEL
ALBUQUERQUE and
MATEUS SANTOLOUCO

**AMERICAN VAMPIRE
VOL. 3**

with RAFAEL
ALBUQUERQUE and
SEAN MURPHY

**AMERICAN VAMPIRE
VOL. 4**

with RAFAEL
ALBUQUERQUE and
JORDI BERNET

*"At a time when vampire stories engulf pop culture,
this one's actually fresh and original."*
— ENTERTAINMENT WEEKLY

AMERICAN VAMPIRE

SCOTT SNYDER   RAFAEL ALBUQUERQUE
and
STEPHEN KING

VERTIGO